LET'S BECOME EMOTIONAL FIRST AIDERS

A guide for parents and children

by Kingsley Ogedengbe

Contents

Worry

Stress

Bullying

Rejection

Sadness

Peer Mentoring

Faskin the Manikin
To find out more, visit *FaskinFirstAid.co.uk*

How to use this book

- -

Integral to loving and enriched relationships between people are **good communication** and **empathy**. Psychological research, which deals with behaviour and the mind, has shown that from the age of two, a child can understand and differentiate between someone else's feelings and their own; in other words, regardless of how they are feeling at the time, they can tell when someone is happy or sad.

This book aims to inspire parents wishing to boost their child's level of confidence, and their ability to determine what to do when someone becomes emotionally hurt. Equipping your child with these skills can also help increase their popularity amongst their family members and school friends. By covering common topics — worry, stress, bullying, rejection, sadness and peer mentoring — your child can be better prepared to deal with these issues should they arise.

I would suggest you **choose a time when your child is feeling talkative and playful**, to bring out this book and read a chapter. You don't need to follow each chapter in order — the book is clearly indexed, allowing you to find and select your topic of choice. You can teach one or several children at a time, although teaching in small groups might be best, where they are of a similar age.

Creating time to talk is so important in helping your child to express their feelings — it also gives you an insight into what they are thinking and how they see things. As their parent you are already an influential figure, but try to avoid using this as an opportunity to criticise or lecture your child. Allow them to feel free to express themselves without being subjected to harsh criticism.

Although, throughout the book, you will be the teacher/introducer, try to avoid making the child feel like they are at school. Keep the chat light and easy — the book guides you with clear objectives and aims. You could mention that *you* are interested in learning new things too! **Above all, keep going with the praise and gratitude** — things like "Hey, that's a really interesting point of view" or "I'm learning so much from us doing this together. Thank you!"

Having a meaningful talk will help your child feel more empowered and appreciated. **As parents, we would like our children to think of us as nurturing, supportive, and good listeners**, so this is a great opportunity to be an example of that, rather than to be simply "Do as I say, not as I do."

Another benefit that comes from working with this book is how it can lead to further discussion of these topics in the future. New challenges and situations are waiting for your child, but, through this book, you can help them deal with those challenges, using the values and principles discussed here. These are things that can contribute to their overall wellbeing, success and happiness.

Faskin the Manikin, featured through the book, is a really helpful aid, especially with remembering. A *Faskin the Manikin* figure is available for purchase, and is a beneficial and useful companion, both to this book, and my *Let's Learn First Aid* book. Children can stick labels on the manikin when discussing topics, which makes things a lot easier to approach and discuss. Having Faskin around *our* home has certainly prompted our children to talk about these topics, and ask questions!

Kingsley Ogedengbe

Introduction to Emotional First Aid

Have you learnt about First Aid? If you have, doesn't it make you feel good about yourself, to know you can help someone in difficulty?

If someone bumps their head, or cuts their leg, we can give them First Aid. We can take care of them until they are better.

However, there are more ways we can help people. Sometimes, people's feelings hurt. Do you think they still need help?

When someone has hurt their emotions we can give what we are going to call **Emotional First Aid**.

If someone is feeling worried or sad, we can think of this as an emotional cut or fracture. We can help them to feel better, just the same as if we help someone who is physically hurt.

The thing is, we can easily tell if someone has hurt part of their body, because we can usually see where they are injured.

With people's feelings it is more difficult to recognise they are hurting. In fact, they might not even know, themselves, what is wrong.

It is important that we learn how to notice if someone is emotionally injured and give them the correct sort of First Aid, so they feel better.

Emotional injuries can often last longer than physical ones — their effects can last for years, so support is very important.

Worry

In this session we are going to:

* learn how to recognise if someone is worried
* recognise how worries can make people feel
* understand that worries are normal and everyone has them
* think about how we can help

AGE 3-5 + 5-7

What is a worry?

A worry is a thought that won't leave your head and keeps bothering you. You might have one in your head right now! It could be you are worried about something that has happened or something that is about to happen.

Let's talk about worries

Think of things that people might worry about. You could talk about a worry of your own to get the discussion rolling — it is important that children understand they are not alone in having worries.

Sometimes, worries can take over our thoughts and make us feel sad, but **they can also help us to make the right choices**. If we worry that doing something is going to make someone upset or sad, we don't do it — we make the right choice.

Is someone worried?

To learn how to help someone who is worried, first let's see **how we can tell if they are**.

They might:

- not be as chatty as they normally are

- get upset and feel sad more than usual

- not want to come to school

- not want to play with anyone at playtime

- not want to eat their snack or lunch

What can we do to help?

If we want to help them with a worry they have, we have to let them know they can talk to us about it. That means we have to be *really good listeners*.

Let's share what makes us good listeners:

- We are interested in what others are saying.

- We don't let ourselves become distracted.

- We don't talk over others.

- We don't rudely interrupt others.

Once we have listened to our friend's worry, we can think about how we can help them.

We could:

- offer to play with them — this might take their mind off it

- share a story with them

- encourage them to draw or write about their worry — this could then be thrown in the bin to 'get rid' of it

- tell them about a time we were worried and what we did to make things better

If we don't know how to help our friend we could get them to **share their worry with someone else**. Who would be a good person they could share their worry with?

Discuss this question and share ideas — answers could include teachers, learning support assistants, parents, siblings, etc.

Faskin says:

It is normal for us to be worried, have doubts and feel anxious at times, but we can control these emotions and thoughts by teaching ourselves to breathe more freely, stay calm, and think of positive outcomes.

AGE 7-11

What is a worry?

A worry is a kind of bad thought that gets stuck in your head. You might not know exactly what it is, but it just bothers you.

Let's talk about worries

Think of some examples of things that might cause a worry — these might include school work, friendships, appearance.

It's normal to think things over — it helps us to keep safe and manage dangers. **Worries can help us organise our ideas so we can make sensible choices and decisions.**

But worries can also take over our thoughts and start to make them really unhappy ones.

There are ways to help someone who is having problems with a worry. First, let's see **how we can tell if a worry is bothering someone.**

Signs of worry might include:

- feeling nervous
- not being able to relax
- getting sad or angry more than usual
- having a sense of impending danger, panic or doom
- feeling weak or tired
- having trouble concentrating or thinking about anything other than one negative thing
- having trouble sleeping

What can we do to help?

You may think someone's worries are quite small or simple, but remember, to them they might seem much bigger. We need to make sure our reaction reassures the person we are helping. We need to **empathise** — that is, to try and see their situation from *their* point of view.

5

If someone cut their head would you just say, "Pull yourself together, it's nothing to worry about"? Of course you wouldn't — you would help them to deal with their injury. It's the same with worries.

We also need to be **good listeners**.

Let's examine the kinds of skills that make us good listeners

- We are interested in what people are saying.

- We don't let ourselves become distracted.

- We don't talk over other people.

- We don't rudely interrupt anyone.

Some effective ways we can give Emotional First Aid

- Let someone share a worry with us — it can make them feel better.

- Encourage them to draw or write about their worry — this could then be thrown in the bin to 'get rid' of it.

- Share an experience we have had of a similar thing.

- Let them know of someone who can give advice that would help with their worry.

Make a list of people someone could talk to if they are worried about something specific such as a piece of work, or maybe something to do with their health.

Stress

In this session we are going to:

* discuss what stress is
* learn about some of the signs of stress
* think about how we can help

AGE 3-5 + 5-7

What is stress?

Children will have heard adults using the word 'stress', probably quite often, but might not know what it means.

People get stressed if they feel they can't do something properly, or might be about to get something wrong.

Take a balloon and write the word 'Stress' on the side. Inflate it a little, and imagine that the air in the balloon represents the feeling of stress. We all feel stress, but it often goes away — release the air.

Inflate the balloon again, but, this time, keep going until the balloon is big. Again, imagine that the air in the balloon is that feeling of stress. What is going to happen if we keep adding stress?

Think about how adding more and more stress can cause problems to people's mental wellbeing, and can make them ill.

Someone might get stressed if they:

- can't get a piece of work right

- upset a friend

- think they might have done something wrong

- are too busy, and there is too much going on

Someone might get stressed because a member of their family is worried about something.

Some of the signs of stress

As Emotional First Aiders, let's look at some of the signs that tell us someone is becoming too stressed. These might include:

- becoming angry or upset

- ignoring a problem

- pretending the stress isn't happening

- not eating properly

- not being able to concentrate

- sleeping too much

The feeling of stress doesn't always last long, and it doesn't stop us enjoying our day. However, like a worry, it can start to grow, and stop us thinking about good things.

It is important that we help people who are feeling stressed, so the feeling doesn't get worse.

How can we help?

Here are some of the things we can do to support someone who is stressed:

- Talk about what is making them stressed — this can be particularly helpful.

- Find something relaxing to do — drawing, or colouring a picture, perhaps.

- Get them to share their stresses with an adult.

- Get them active — running and jumping outside can get rid of stress.

- Find them a quiet place where they can just relax.

- Share a story.

Faskin says:

When we feel nervous and uncomfortable about changes or new things about to happen in our lives, we experience stress. We can calm ourselves by closing our eyes and breathing slowly.

AGE **7-11**

What is stress?

Children will have heard adults using the word stress, probably quite often, but might not know what it means.

People get stressed if they feel they can't do something properly, or might be about to get something wrong.

Take a balloon and write the word 'Stress' on the side. Inflate it a little, and imagine that the air in the balloon represents the feeling of stress. We all feel stress, but it often goes away — release the air.

Inflate the balloon again, but, this time, keep going until the balloon is big. Again, imagine that the air in the balloon is that feeling of stress. What is going to happen if we keep adding stress?

Think about how adding more and more stress can cause problems to people's mental wellbeing, and can make them ill.

Our bodies are designed to cope with stress. When we are stressed, our bodies release adrenalin to help us, **but they can't cope if adrenalin keeps getting released**. If that happens, it can lower the power of our immune system, which makes it harder for our bodies to fight infection.

Someone might get stressed if they:

- have lots of work to do
- are preparing for a test
- can't get on with friends or family
- think they are always making mistakes
- are too busy, and there is too much going on

Someone might get stressed because a member of their family is worried about something.

Some of the signs of stress

As Emotional First Aiders, let's look at some of the signs that tell us someone is becoming too stressed. These might include:

- becoming angry or upset

- ignoring a problem

- pretending the stress isn't happening

- not eating properly

- not being able to concentrate

- sleeping too much

- continually getting ill

The feeling of stress doesn't always last long, and it doesn't stop us enjoying our day. However, like a worry, it can start to grow, and stop us thinking about good things.

It is important that we help people who are feeling stressed, so the feeling doesn't get worse.

How can we help?

Here are some things we can do to support someone who is stressed:

- Talk about what is making them stressed — this can be particularly helpful.

- Find something relaxing to do — drawing, or colouring a picture, perhaps.

- Get them to share their stresses with a trusted adult.

- Get them active — doing sports can relieve stress.

- Find them a quiet place where they can just relax.

- Encourage them to listen to some music to help them relax.

- Help them to organise their time better, so they can get their work finished.

Bullying

In this session we are going to:

* understand what bullying is
* learn about how it feels to be bullied
* think about how we can help

AGE 3-5

What is bullying?

To explain what bullying is, let's use toys x and y to set up a situation.

We're going to imagine that toy x is playing with something, and toy y comes and snatches it away. That's not nice is it?

Every day that toy x comes in to play with something, toy y takes it off them.

If someone keeps being nasty or unkind to somebody else, this is called bullying, and the person doing it is called a bully.

Sometimes they might be unkind to someone because of what they are wearing, or the colour of their hair, or who they play with.

Bullying can make people feel so sad that they don't want to come to

school, or they don't want to go out at playtime. Sometimes it can stop them wanting to eat their lunch or snack.

How can we help?

As Emotional First Aiders it is important that we know how to help people who are being bullied. We can:

● tell a teacher or learning support assistant — they can deal with the problem straightaway

● offer to go with the person being bullied to tell an adult — they might be scared to go on their own. If you offer to help, it might make it easier for them.

● tell the bully that what they are doing is unkind, and ask them how they would feel if someone did that to them

● let the person being bullied know that they are not alone, and invite them to join our games

● remind them they are a special member of the class

● try to involve the bully in our games — they might be being unkind because they are lonely, but don't know how to make friends

AGE **5-7** **+** **7-11**

What is bullying?

Bullying is when someone (the bully) keeps being nasty or unkind to others, using 'power' they have over them to try to hurt or upset them, again and again.

Sometimes they might be unkind to someone because of what they are wearing, or the colour of their hair, or who they play with or hang around with.

Bullying doesn't just happen at school — people can be bullied online as well. This can often make the person being bullied feel even worse because they can't see a way to escape from it.

The challenge for Emotional First Aiders is that friends might not always tell people they are being bullied. Why do you think this might be?

Signs to look out for of someone being bullied

● Are they reluctant to come into school?

● Are they being left out of things, or not invited to play games?

● Do they stay away from others at lunch and breaktimes?

Bullying

- Do they try to avoid being in situations like the toilets, communal areas or changing rooms?

- Have you heard people saying things about them that are not true?

How can we help?

As Emotional First Aiders it is important that we know how to help people who are being bullied. We can:

- tell a teacher or learning support assistant — they can deal with the problem straightaway

- offer to go with the person being bullied, to tell an adult — they might be scared to go on their own. If you offer to help, it might make it easier for them.

- tell the bully that what they are doing is unkind, and ask them how they would feel if someone did that to them

- let the person being bullied know that they are not alone, and invite them to join our games and conversations

- talk to them about how they are feeling — let them know we are there to help them

- remind them that they are a special member of the class, and of their special qualities

- try to involve the bully in our games and conversations — they might be being unkind

Bullies often like to pick on people that are smaller, weaker and quieter than themselves. If you see someone being nasty towards someone else it's important to tell an adult or teacher straightaway.

because they are lonely, but don't know how to make friends

- make it clear to the person being bullied that it is not their fault

Bullying can have a big impact on someone's mental wellbeing. No-one has the right to make someone else feel bad about themselves, lonely, or sad.

Bullying

Rejection

In this session we are going to:

* understand what rejection means

* learn to recognise why someone might feel rejected

* think about how we can help someone who is left out

AGE 3-5 + 5-7

What is rejection?

To explain what rejection means, let's try a simple exercise.

Gather five toys on the floor and explain that the toys are each being given a sticker for getting all their spellings correct (for example). Hand the stickers out to all but one of the toys. Explain that one toy can't have a sticker because it didn't get all its spellings correct this week.

Discuss how that toy might feel — things like feeling sad, lonely, etc.

Next, line the toys up and explain that they have been training for a race, with the first four to finish going to the Toy Olympics. Pick a different toy this time, and explain that this one can't go because it came last in the race.

14

Faskin says:

Rejection can feel like a pain in the heart or stomach — our brain reacts as though it's been physically hurt. It can help if you accept what has happened and move onto something new.

Again, share how that toy might feel — things like lonely, and left out.

This experience, of missing out on something, is called rejection.

There are lots of situations where someone might experience rejection. These might include:

- not being chosen for a sports team

- not being chosen to do a job for the teacher

- not getting a sticker/award/ certificate

- not being given a part in a school play

Share your own experiences of this.

Everyone experiences rejection at times, even teachers and parents.

As Emotional First Aiders, we need to find ways to help others who are feeling rejected. This will include being **good listeners**, which means:

- we are interested in what others are saying

- we don't let ourselves become distracted

- we don't talk over others

- we don't rudely interrupt others

How can we help?

- Tell them to not give up — if they keep trying, they will get better.

- Help them to see what they are good at — we can't be good at *everything*, but we are all good at *something*.

- Help them to get better at something — you might be able to show them how to do this.

AGE 7-11

What is rejection?

Find images of J.K. Rowling, Lady Gaga, Ian Wright and Colonel Harland David Sanders. **These famous people all experienced rejection before they found success.**

J.K. Rowling, author of the *Harry Potter* stories, was not an instant success. Her first book, *Harry Potter and the Philosopher's Stone*, was rejected by twelve major publishers, yet, to date, this book has sold more than 100 million copies.

Lady Gaga was told she would never make it as a singer because of her looks. To date, she has sold 27 million albums and 146 million singles.

Ian Wright, television presenter and former professional footballer, played 581 league games, scoring 387 goals for top teams like Arsenal and Crystal Palace. He also earned 33 caps for England. As a child, he was rejected by many teams, but, despite all these setbacks, never gave up. He was eventually signed by Crystal Palace, at 22 years old.

Colonel Harland David Sanders is famous for creating the fast-food brand KFC. His special recipe for fried chicken was rejected over 1000 times by restaurants before finally being accepted. Today there are over 23,000 KFC outlets in 140 countries.

Discuss an experience of when you felt rejected.

This could include:

- not being chosen for a sports team
- not being chosen to do a job for the teacher
- not getting a sticker/award/ certificate
- not being given a part in a school play

As Emotional First Aiders it's important that we recognise the emotions people might have about rejection and how we can support them.

Often, with feelings of rejection, someone can give up on something they enjoy doing. **This can lead to them feeling isolated and alone, and can be detrimental to their mental wellbeing.**

How can we help?

Here are some steps we can take to support someone who feels rejected

- Identify things they could do to improve for next time.
- Point out what they are good at.
- Help them to get better at something — this might be something you can do, or perhaps you can identify someone else who can help.
- Advise them not to give up — *'If at first you don't succeed...'*

There's also something else you can use to support someone in this situation — it's called *resilience*.

Resilience is another word for the inner strength that keeps us going, even when things get really challenging. You could use the idea of resilience to reassure someone that the rejection they feel will actually make them stronger.

Try this role-play

One of you takes on the role of one of the above celebrities. The other plays the Emotional First Aider, who has to decide how to give advice and encouragement to the celebrity, to help them deal with their rejection.

Sadness

In this session we are going to:

* understand what makes people sad
* learn how to recognise if someone is sad
* think about how we can help someone cope with sadness

AGE 3-5 + 5-7

What makes people sad?

Think about the different things that can make someone feel sad. Think about why they feel like that and how long they might feel sad for.

For example, if someone has bumped their leg and it soon feels better, their feeling of sadness might go away quickly. If, on the other hand, they have lost something that is very special to them, the sadness could last a lot longer.

It's OK to feel sad — it can help us to cope with things.

How do people show they are sad?

There are many different signs that

can tell us someone is feeling sad. These include:

- crying
- wanting to be left alone
- feeling poorly with a headache or a funny tummy
- not eating their snack or lunch
- not smiling or laughing at things that would normally make them happy
- feeling tired

How can we help someone feel better when they are sad?

We can:

- talk to them about how they are feeling
- encourage them to share their feelings with an adult
- involve them in a game we're playing
- share a story
- ask them to help us do something — maybe it is something they are really good at
- share a funny joke that you know
- draw them a colourful picture

If they still can't lose their feeling of sadness, we can **let them know we are always ready to listen** if they feel like it. We can also tell an adult, because they might be able to give them the help they need.

AGE 7-11

What makes people sad?

Think about the different things that can make someone feel sad. Share your own experiences of feeling sad.

If someone is feeling *really* sad, or it lasts a long time, this can lead to feelings of **depression** which can become a **serious risk to their mental wellbeing**.

It's OK to feel sad — it can help us to cope with things. It can help us to become more resilient to challenges we may face later on in our lives.

How do people show they are sad?

People can show they are sad in different ways. Signs that might tell us someone is feeling sad include:

- not wanting to do things that they previously enjoyed

Feeling sad is a natural emotion that all people experience at some point in their lives. The good thing is that if we decide to change our thinking it can disappear.

- not wanting to meet up with friends, or avoiding situations

- sleeping more, or less, than normal

- eating more, or less, than normal

- feeling irritable, upset, miserable or lonely

- being self-critical

- feeling tired and not having any energy

How can we help someone feel better when they are sad?

We can:

- talk to them about how they are feeling

- encourage them to share their feelings with a trusted adult

- involve them in something we're doing

- ask them to help us do something — maybe it's something they're really good at

- do something kind for them

- emphasise all the things that make them special

- share something funny with them

- get them active — playing a sport or dancing to music, for example

If they still can't lose their feeling of sadness, we can let them know we are always ready to listen if they feel like it. **Talking is a really good way to help someone deal with sadness.**

If they stay sad, and we are worried about them, we can tell a trusted adult so they can talk to them about it.

Sadness

Peer Mentoring

In this session we are going to:

* understand what peer mentoring is
* learn what makes a good peer mentor
* think about how we can help as a peer mentor

AGE 3-5 + 5-7 + 7-11

What is peer mentoring?

If someone hurts themselves, physically, we can help them with First Aid. If we know First Aid, we can even tell an adult what to do!

We can do a similar thing using Emotional First Aid. We can help someone, or we can show someone else how to help.

When we show someone, in our school or at home, how to do something, we become a kind of teacher, known as a **peer mentor**. As a peer mentor, by showing what we have learned, we can be a role model for others.

If we all learn how to do the right thing, our schools will become safer and more caring places to learn in.

Let's think about the qualities we need, to be a peer mentor.

We need to:

- be friendly when someone needs our help
- know how to help
- know who to go to if we can't help
- be able to understand how someone is feeling — this is called **empathy**

There is one more important quality — we need to be able to control our own emotions and feelings. This means if something isn't going our way we can't just give up or get angry. We have to think calmly about what we need to do, and work out how to do it.

How can we help?

If we see someone who needs Emotional First Aid there are things we can say and do, whatever they are struggling with. We can:

- listen to what they say, so we can understand what is wrong. Good listening skills include:

  ▶ being interested in what others are saying

  ▶ not letting ourselves become distracted

  ▶ not talking over other people

  ▶ not rudely interrupting them

Faskin says:

Being a peer mentor is like being someone's best friend. Making someone feel better by being supportive and friendly can make such a difference to how they see things.

- choose the right way to support them
- find someone to help them if we can't help
- use positive words to help them feel better
- be a friend if they need one

Sometimes, someone might not want our help, and that's OK. We can't force our help on them. What we *can* do is let them know we are ready to help if they need us — even if just for a chat.

CPSIA information can be obtained
at www.ICGtesting.com
Printed in the USA
BVHW022019011020
590105BV00012B/160

9 781838 185312